Change-Maker Village

Change-Maker Village

by Mel Kappin Blume

Dedication

To Mandisa Norward, thank you for sharing your beautiful name
with our brave girl.

To my brilliant Mom, who embarks upon every roller coaster ride with me,
questioning me every step of the way. You make me a better writer, storyteller
and person, and I'll never be able to truly express my immense gratitude.
Thank you, my special Dear.

To my sunshine-filled Dad, thank you for your endless optimism. Your energy
alone could light up the world. Love you and Mom to the moon.

To my family, near and far, thanks for your limitless love. I can feel every hug,
even if we're 3,000 miles away.

And lastly, to my husband and kids. Thanks for putting up with a 24/7
writer-wife and -mom. You are the greatest humans and bring me more joy
than you could ever imagine. My love expands to new dimensions with you.

Read. Listen. Donate. Vote.

~ Mel Kaspin Blume

Once Upon a Blume, LLC
This book has been published in the United States of America by
Once Upon a Blume, LLC
1990 S. Bundy Drive, Suite 450
Los Angeles, CA 90025
onceuponablume.com
@onceuponablume

Second Printing.

Copyright ©2020 Mel Kaspin Blume

All rights reserved. No part of this publication may be reproduced in any form or by any means, electronic or mechanical, including photocopying, recording or by any information storage and retrieval system, without permission in writing from the publisher Once Upon a Blume, LLC.

For more information, address: inquiries@onceuponablume.com.

Publishing director: JinJa Davis-Birkenbeuel

Book design and production by JinJa Birkenbeuel, Birk Creative (@birkcreative)
Art direction by JinJa Birkenbeuel, Birk Creative
Illustrations by Lisa Aihara (@lisaaihara)

"400 years" Lyrics by Mel Kaspin Blume; Music by Brian Blake and JinJa Davis-Birkenbeuel

Printed in the United States of America.
Published by Once Upon a Blume, LLC
ISBN: 978-1-7359664-9-6

"400 YEARS"

Open your ears and your heart.
For change to have a chance to start.
The differences are clear.
Listen. And you'll hear.
It started over 400 years ago,
and hurts more than you'll ever know.
Open your ears. Open your heart.
For change to have a chance to start.

Mel Kaspin Blume

Foreword

The year 2020 has been one of incredible strife, confusion, disappointment and rage within me. Amidst the ruins, I found hope. I found and created beauty, art and vibrant collaborations among free spirits—artists, songwriters and entrepreneurs.

I met author Mel Kaspin Blume after I read her sincere plea for change in a passionate post on a social media channel. I remember at the time feeling overwhelmed by the volume of startling admissions of innocent ignorance by so many white people on the channel. Mel's public proclamation that she intended to work on herself to begin to try to change race relations spoke to me. Although I did not know Mel, I asked in a reply to go beyond giving charity to Black people. I asked her instead to *fight* for financial justice and freedom for Black women.

Mel wrote back to me with a request for a conversation about a collaboration, which culminated in her book *Change-Maker Village*. The book is based on her life as a Jewish girl growing up thinking Black people had equality, and realizing now, with shame, that the narrative "everyone is equal" was a lie, that she believed.

Our collaboration on an anti-racist and pro-Black book for children was a dream come true for me. In this process, I became Mel's publishing director, entrepreneurial coach, co-writer (of her song "400 Years"), graphic designer and finally art director for the book's characters developed and illustrated by the amazing Lisa Aihara.

I'm overjoyed to work with a woman who champions collaborative freedom and refuses to hoard knowledge and access. Trust is a big requirement to be successful at anything. Women, especially Black women like me, have to prove their value and excellence almost every step of the way. With Mel during the creation of this book I found a creative relationship where trust was assumed and didn't need to be earned.

Thank you, Mel. I'm excited to be on this magnificent journey with you. Let's change the world!

JinJa Davis-Birkenbeuel

Hi! My name is **Rose**.

I'm in **fourth grade** and feeling sad.

Pretty soon, I'm going to Capitol Hall Middle School.

And my **best friend** and next-door neighbor, **Mandisa**, will be going to Grove Middle School.

There is an invisible line between our homes that sends us to two **different** middle schools.

I've never been apart from Disa before.

Even our **moms** are doctors at the same hospital!

We're like **sisters**.

We both **love** arts and crafts, going to the library and laughing at silly jokes!

The only **difference** is that Disa has black skin and I have white skin.

Oh, and she plays the piano and sings.

Today is Saturday, and Disa and I walk to the new art store that just opened around the corner.

As we walk in, we are welcomed by **rainbow-colored** paints and cool pottery.

Disa spots a ready-to-paint mini piano and my eyes land on a ready-to-paint **heart**.

"Woo-hoo! Rose, this is such an **amazing** store!" says Disa with her contagious **smile**.

"I know! I'm so glad we found it!" I exclaim with a grin as we **high-five**.

At the front counter, I pay for my heart and **pink** paint with my take-out-the-garbage allowance, and Disa pays for her piano and **black** and white paint with her take-out-the-garbage allowance. As we're walking out of the store, a loud security **alarm rings**.

Disa quickly drops her bag, stretches her arms to the sky, and shouts, "I am 9 years old and my name is Mandisa."

I freeze. "Disa, what? What are you doing?"

What is happening?

"Be quiet, Rose." Disa is staring straight ahead, her face wearing a serious expression I have never seen before.

A lady who **looks like my grandma** runs out of the store. "What did you take?" she **screams** at Disa with **angry eyes**. She grabs Disa's shopping bag from the sidewalk.

Disa, calm and serious, says with her arms still up, "I didn't take anything."

My **heart pounds**.

"Leave her alone!" I cry.

A second later, a younger lady comes running out of the store. "Mom, get inside!" she says in a stern voice as she takes Disa's bag back and returns it to her.

"Girls, I'm so sorry. This store is new and we're still figuring out the alarm system. Please enjoy your new art and I hope to see you again soon."

Disa and I walk away in **silence**. My chest hurts **thinking** about how she feels right now. Then I ask Disa, "Why didn't that lady ask me if I stole anything?"

"That **angry lady** is one of millions of people

who think Black people are less than them.

Black people have never been treated **equally**,

even after **slavery** ended."

I blink back **tears**. I didn't realize Disa could ever

experience **racism**. I ask another question.

"Why did you put your arms up like that?"

"My **parents told me to** do that when I was six, so nobody tries to hurt me and so they can see that I'm cooperating."

I stay silent. It makes me **feel so sad** to think that Disa was only six when her parents taught her this.

It makes me feel sad I hadn't thought about how life might be **different for her** because of her skin color.

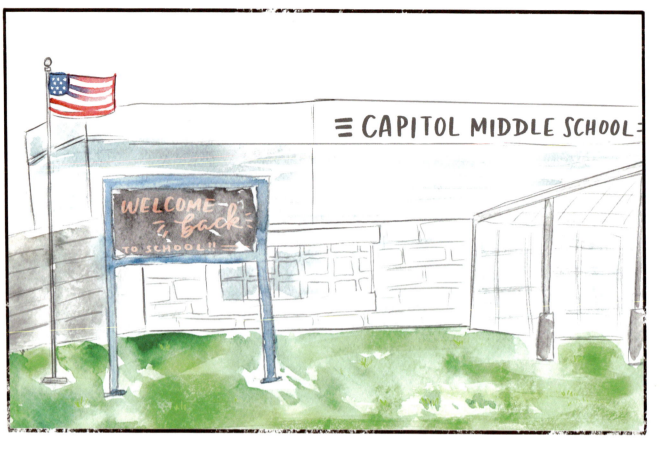

Disa continues, "Rose, look at the schools we're going to next year. Capitol Hall has mostly students with white skin, and it's **beautiful**, with brand new everything! Grove has mostly Black students, and is **run down**. They don't even have a music program."

I keep listening to my friend. I knew the schools looked different, but I hadn't really thought about why. Now **I wish** I had paid more attention.

My mind races in circles. I feel like everything I learned in school about racial equality was a lie.

Disa shares, "I've heard about things like this happening, but it never happened to me before. Racism has to end, Rose. We need to do something to stop this."

"Yes, we do. Right now." I say with my whole heart.

"It'll take a lot, but we could start with a first step," says Disa.

Disa and I **sit** on the front steps of her house and **talk** about what we can do, as **9-year-olds**, to make a difference.

That night, Disa and I, **together**, create something **awesome**.

The next day, our **parents** help us **create** fliers and we put them up all over town. My dad even emails it to our school principal.

Saturday comes quickly. All morning our families set up blankets, tables and chairs on our front lawns, and we create a little reading nook for the library books we borrowed including *Let's Talk About Race* and *I Am Human*.

Disa's Dad's friend offered to come and speak to our neighborhood about the National Association for the Advancement of Colored People (NAACP), a **civil rights** organization that works to end racism and makes sure everyone is treated equally.

Disa and I feel so much **joy** when we see the size of the crowd. About a hundred people with dark skin, light skin and every shade in between come to our Change-Maker Village.

My **favorite part** of the day is performing Disa's song. I join Disa in her living room, as the guests gather outside. The windows are open wide, and my friend sits down on her piano bench, her **royal throne**.

She plays a new song she has written called, "400 Years." The **powerful** lyrics capture every pair of ears on the lawn.

"Open your ears and your heart. For change to have a chance to start. The differences are clear. Listen. And you'll hear. It started over 400 years ago. And it hurts more than you'll ever know. Open your ears and your heart. For change to have a chance to start."

I recognize the art store owner and see that she brought her mom. I'm **glad** they accepted the invitation we taped on the door of the art store.

At first, silence is the only sound heard as we finish the last note. Then, the crowd shares a **booming applause** that makes us smile—big.

Disa and I walk together to her porch.

We both face the crowd from her front steps.

"Thank you for listening to my song. Please, please **continue to listen**," says Disa.

"Listen to what Black people have to say. We need change. Racism needs to stop. **Hate needs to stop.** Please join us as change-makers," I say.

"Disa and I thought of a change-maker **pledge**, and if you'd like, repeat after us." Together we say, "I will **speak up** when something feels wrong. I will listen. I will **spread kindness**, respect and love. Every single day."

To our surprise, the entire lawn of guests, including the mom of the store owner, repeats these words.

Disa says, "Rose and I have a certificate for you. We **can** create change. I know we can. But we need ears, eyes and voices to make it happen."

Disa and I say,

"We can do it. Together."

I AM A Change-Maker CERTIFICATE

_____

YOUR NAME GOES HERE

I CAN DO ANYTHING

I WILL SPEAK UP WHEN SOMETHING FEELS WRONG. I WILL LISTEN. I WILL SPREAD KINDNESS, RESPECT, AND LOVE. EVERY DAY.

HOW YOU CAN HELP RIGHT NOW

- Remind your parents to ~VOTE~
- Listen to your Black friends, family, and community members.
- Give money to helpful organizations like the National Association for the Advancement of Colored People (NAACP)
- Read books like "I AM HUMAN" and "The Story of Ruby Bridges"
- Treat everyone with kindness and respect
- Spread LOVE ♥
- Repeat after me: "I can do anything!"

How Your Grown-Ups Can Help Right Now:

VOTE.
Vote, vote, vote, vote.

DONATE.*
The Loveland Foundation | thelovelandfoundation.org
American Civil Liberties Union | aclu.org/issues/racial-justice
Justice for Breonna Taylor | gofundme.com/f/9v4q2-justice-for-breonna-taylor
National Bail Fund Network | communityjusticeexchange.org/nbfn-directory
Know Your Rights Camp | knowyourrightscamp.com/who-we-are?form=KnowYourRightsCamp
The Conscious Kid | theconsciouskid.org/donate
GirlTrek | girltrek.org
Campaign Zero | joincampaignzero.org/#vision

*The Change-Maker Village Team is in no way affiliated with any of the organizations and receive nothing from the organizations if a reader or parent chooses to donate. Different organizations support different things and use donations for different services or resources. Find one that is right for you by researching any organizations that you might like to donate to and see if their mission is in line with what you want to support. These are some of our suggestions.

For more information and organizations: nymag.com/strategist/article/where-to-donate-for-black-lives-matter.html

READ.
A resource for grown-ups:
rachel-cargle.com/elizabeths-bookshop-writing-centre

A resource for kids:
teacherspayteachers.com/Product/Diverse-Book-List-5638016

LISTEN.

Author's Note

I wrote a book, based on the friendship of a white girl and a Black girl, and there's no age range. Because, everyone has the power to create change. As a white Jew, I removed my privileged lens to see the truth, and stand in solidarity with and for Black people, with my entire being.

This is something that rips my soul when I think about it, but I didn't know that many Black parents teach their kids, at a very young age, to raise their hands above their heads to cooperate with the police. I didn't know about the Tulsa Race Massacre, I didn't know about Juneteenth, and I didn't know about redlining.

Now that I do know, I'll never stop fighting for change. We need to make sure the freedom white people celebrate rings true for everyone in this country.

Black people, brown people, people of every shade on the outside, need to be seen, and heard, and protected. No one should wake up and go to sleep living in fear. Please, vote.

As President Barack Obama famously said, "We are the ones we've been waiting for. We are the change that we seek."

A massive thank you to the *Change-Maker Village* team. You are geniuses.

Thank you, JinJa, for having faith in me to join me on this journey. Your faith was the force that drove me to do this. I'm forever grateful to have met you. You shared your expertise and took the story far past any of my daydreams. Your talent, drive and passion can change the world. Thank you, thank you, brilliant JinJa.

To my unicorn illustrator Lisa, thank you, for bringing this story to life. Your dedication to creating our hopeful and fierce girls, and their world, in the most magnetic way far exceeded all expectations. I love Disa and Rose and can't wait for the world to meet them! Thank you, friend. For everything.

I am insanely grateful to you both and everyone else who joined us on this journey: Amy Cohen, Lenoria Addison, Brian Blake, Alix Reid, Margie Schulz and Meredith Esarey.

Thank you from the bottom of my heart. Read. Listen. Donate. Vote.

To change,
Mel Kaspin Blume

Footnotes

Tulsa Race Massacre: The Greenwood District in Tulsa, Oklahoma, was called "Black Wall Street" in the 1920s. After an elevator incident between a white woman and Black man, an angry white mob looted, burned, and destroyed 35 square blocks of businesses and houses in Greenwood. Hundreds were killed and left homeless, and this riot was left out of newspapers and history books and not acknowledged in schools. – Alicia Lee and Sara Sidner, "99 years ago today, America was shaken by one of its deadliest acts of racial violence," *CNN.com.* June 1, 2020, *https://www.cnn.com/2020/06/01/us/tulsa-race-massacre-1921-99th-anniversary-trnd/index.html*

Juneteenth: "On June 19, 1865, enslaved African-Americans in Galveston, Texas, were told they were free… [This] announcement put into effect the Emancipation Proclamation, which had been issued more than two and a half years earlier on Jan. 1, 1863, by President Abraham Lincoln." – Derrick Bryson Taylor, "So You Want to Learn About Juneteenth?," *Nytimes.com.* June 19, 2020, *https://www.nytimes.com/article/juneteenth-day-celebration.html*

Redlining: "In 1933… the federal government began a program…designed to increase—and segregate—America's housing stock…African-Americans and other people of color were left out of the new suburban communities. [Author Richard Rothstein] notes that the Federal Housing Administration… furthered the segregation efforts by refusing to insure mortgages in and near African-American neighborhoods—a policy known as "redlining." Rothstein says these decades-old housing policies have had a lasting effect on American society." – Terry Gross, "A 'Forgotten History' Of How The U.S. Government Segregated America," *Npr.org.* May, 3 2017, *https://www.npr.org/2017/05/03/526655831/a-forgotten-history-of-how-the-u-s-government-segregated-america*

Book design and production by JinJa Birkenbeuel, Birk Creative (@birkcreative)
Art direction by JinJa Birkenbeuel, Birk Creative
Publishing director and business coach: JinJa Birkenbeuel
"400 years" Lyrics by Mel Kaspin Blume; Music by Brian Blake and JinJa Davis-Birkenbeuel
Illustrations by Lisa Aihara (@lisaaihara)